Impressions

Dr. Paul T. M. Jackson

A Publication of The Poetry Box®

Original Cover Art by Fran Bowerbank.
Editing & Book Design by Shawn Aveningo Sanders.
Cover Design by Robert R. Sanders.

ISBN: 978-1-948461-02-3
Printed in the United States of America.

Published by The Poetry Box®, 2018
Beaverton, Oregon
ThePoetryBox.com

For Cécile (Ζωή καί ψυχή)

and Camille (pour que toi aussi tu trouves ton 'poetic eye')

Contents

Impressions on England:

Impressions on Wales:

Impressions on Africa:

Impressions on Ecuador:

Introduction

Some people see things in a certain way. Some people, when they see something, feel compelled to somehow capture it, whether that be by a sketch, a painting, or even a symphony. Chekhov, for instance, while writing *A Journey to Sakhalin*, admitted to this compulsion. The poet William Barnes coined the term, the 'poetic eye.' In one of his poems, The Young Rhymer Snubbed, he writes, "But then my heart did kindle wi' the fleäme o't, // Whenever I did zee a touchen zight, // An' I did all but lose my wits there-right." Barnes would be so moved by the things he saw that he had to put pen to paper and capture it in a poem. I know how he feels. I am one of these people. I see things and I see a poem. I want to somehow capture, not so much the scene, but the moment, what I felt and thought in that moment, and what that moment meant to me.

Impressions is a small collection of poems inspired by such moments, whether they occurred while cycling through Provence, rambling in Wales, trekking through Galicia, hunting for castles in Corsica, or even on a pirogue in the Amazon. I hope you enjoy sharing these moments with me, and I hope that they help you find your own 'poetic eye.'

An' zoo I vound my friends think all the seäme o't,
That rhyme won't vill the pocket over tight,
But then my heart did kindle wi' the fleäme o't,
Whenever I did zee a touchen zight,
An' I did all but lose my wits there-right.
'Tis likely I shall meäke a losen geäme o't,
But still, ageän, to lighten off the bleäme o't,
Vor all do keep me poor, it still will bring
My heart a pleasure that do leäve noo sting.

~ From William Barnes' "The Young Rhymer Snubbed"

Impressions

The Camargue

Drifting lazily along,
The waters sitting still,
Passing reedy, willowed banks,
Under bridge, around hill.

Old towns rise and fall away,
The sun's always on our backs,
Flamingos pink, horses white,
Long-horned bulls all jet-black.

Reillanne

Before that knoll where Reillanne sits high,
Hills roll away and fields lie wide,
Here haystacks are heaped beneath blue skies,
Golden bundles now summer's arrived.

Elsewhere grasses sway from left to right,
But here it's these bales that catch your eye
Where cattle graze and swallows squeal by,
Throughout the scarecrows and butterflies.

But how did these bales come to lie,
Heaped up high beneath these broad, blue skies?
And who stacked that hay up to such heights,
And left no grass swaying from side to side?

You never see hay being piled high,
Only once gathered and left aside,
Here where hills roll and fields lie wide,
Where cattle graze and swallows squeal by.

Gréolières

Long ago the folk came on down
To that brow way over there,
But today I'm going on up,
And climbing those stony stairs.

At dawn of day I head up as
Dewy glass glistens in groves,
Gossamer sparkles in the sun,
As I ramble, roam, and rove.

I leave behind those sun-drenched heaths,
Leave those dipping downs below,
Those leas and meads are left behind,
And those sweeping dips aglow.

Through woodland ways I briskly stride,
Where rooks roost in lofty trees,
With treetops swaying overhead,
Those well-birded canopies.

Through shady glade and sunny copse,
With foxglove and hose-in-hose,
Through grassy dell and leafy dene,
Where brooks-a-gurgling go.

Butterflies gently flutter by,
And damselflies dance and dart,
A woodpecker smites some elm tree,
And swallow wings're spread apart.

Through open gates and over stiles,
Up onto that raised terrace,
'Round knap and knoll I wend my way,
And heaped-up hillocks I pass.

Here are the ruins of yesteryear,
Which Nature is taking back,
Through ivy-grip and mossy-hold
Walls lay strewn with gaping cracks.

Over there, stood on heathered heath,
La Chapelle Sainte Pétronille,
Abandoned like all the others,
No longer its bell peels.

My path goes on past mere and tarn,
And deep millponds bound by sedge,
'Tween parrocks sitting tight and snug,
With flowery, herby edge.

I break through brambles and briars,
And burst through the tall bulrush,
Hawthorn's here, golden gorse there, and
Underfoot, dandelions are crushed.

Behind, mountains stand proud and tall,
Eagles screech up on the crags,
For dark, air-swimming clouds sweep in,
Which a thyme-breeze wind stream drags.

Up here there are no rosebuds,
Up here, no bleating goats,
But up here, I go a-treading,
Though long deserted by folk.

And behold, that waterfall there,
Crashing down o'er rocky steps,
Tumbling down as white as hoarfrost,
Before winter's grip arrests.

But now the ev'ning's creeping in,
And daylight starts to move on,
Soon owls will hoot and toads will croak,
Once the cicadas have gone.

So as dusk falls and dull twilight sets,
Swiftly back down I must go,
Past those old abodes, blackberry groves,
Dancing nimbly, to and fro.

And my old dog is after me,
His tail wagging, swishing so,
With so much bliss and so much mirth,
After our brisk, daily stroll.

Elsewhere they have pink flamingos,
Elsewhere, black bulls, white horses,
Elsewhere barrows and stone circles,
Great dolmens and tall henges.

But I have *sheilings* and heaped-up cairns,
La Chapelle Sainte Pétronille,
And I have these eagled mountains,
And it's quite enough for me.

Coaraze

We make our way through willowed woods,
A narrow gorge between tall peaks,
I hear the rustling of the leaves,
And the leaf-laden boughs all creak.

I hear the burbling of a brook,
See the oasis through those logs,
Of pools of clear water, full
Of little, wiggling pollywogs.

We struggled along to this spot,
Hidden deep down in the ravine,
But now we sail to the stars,
On a rosemary-scented breeze.

Caussols Again, or Back to Caussols

Up those rocky, winding ways,
Up to those windswept peaks,
Up where the wild beasts tread their paths,
And the world stretches out beneath.

Here the heathered hills lie bare,
Here are those rock-strewn plains,
Here are the trails, and there the tracks,
Which I've come up again.

Then the darkness closes in,
Then the heavens groan,
Then the lightning flashes down,
And I'm here all alone.

Now the wind comes whipping in,
Now it whistles through the trees,
Now the cold is taking hold,
And I drop down to my knees.

Next, those noises of the night,
Next, the howl of wolves,
Next, a scary shriek out there,
And the hooting of owls.

It's not for the fainthearted here,
Nor the lily-livered,
Mountaintops are harsh and cruel,
And helplessly, I shiver.

But there's a starry sky above,
There's a moon rising,
There the magic starts to unfold,
This is the silver lining.

For mountain heights are cold and bleak,
And leave you feeling small,
But underneath the heavens there,
You only stand in awe.

Bézaudun

Cowbells ringing in the woods,
On my way to Bézaudun,
Spring is in the air again,
As I go to Bézaudun.

Kites are in their wakes up there,
On my way to Bézaudun,
Bluebell, crocus, left and right,
As I go to Bézaudun.

All is quiet, all is calm,
On my way to Bézaudun,
So I smile, so blessed am I,
As I go to Bézaudun.

Arcachon

O Arcachon, O Arcachon,
Whose sandy dunes go on and on,
With an ocean of blue before,
And endless seas of green behind,
Open-mouthed, but with bated breath,
I prepare myself to climb.

O Arcachon, O Arcachon,
Whose pine forest flows on and on,
With waves crashing down white o'er there,
And golden grains falling away below,
The wind whips 'gainst my face, and takes
My breath away as I go.

O Arcachon, O Arcachon,
Whose heaped-up piles look proudly on,
There're some who roll rocks up ridges,
And elsewhere spires that reach for skies,
But I look down and away, o'er
Heavenly lands with heavenly eyes.

Occi

Along a rocky, winding way,
Lizards scrambling from our path,
Breaking through blackberry brambles,
The sun beating upon our backs.

Past that old, overhanging oak,
Where we rest in welcome shade,
Then onwards and upwards we go,
To where Occi had been laid.

We find only a ghost town now,
A turquoise bay far below,
With only butterflies fluttering by,
For Guidiceli left long ago.

A chapel is still standing strong,
But its bell no longer rings,
Only the screeching kites are heard,
Lamenting the transience of things.

Even the songbirds lie quiet,
And the silence echoes loud,
The fields lie barren all around,
Which once would have been ploughed.

Built and abandoned by mankind,
This town died long ago,
Nature's since been taking back hold,
Its fingers creeping up from below.

Lama

As summer's sun sets and nighttime falls,
As bats take to wing and nightingales call,
Eventide creeps in, in twilight crawls,
Dusk's shawl opens and takes hold of all.

A tree silhouetted against the sky,
And this village nestled against the hillside,
Clinging to the cliffs, lest down they slide,
Snuggling to the slopes, closing their eyes.

But up there, the sun's chased by the moon,
Whose pale light comes to take away this gloom,
To drown out the Sandman's sleepy tune,
As down from above its pallid light's strewn.

And the evening star shines up there too,
Casting light into that deep blue hue,
To guide the shepherds amidst dark blue,
And light up the sky, for me and for you.

Cinque Terre

As the sun sinks below the sea,
To leave reds and pinks behind,
Shepherds are leading down their flocks,
And fishers draw in their lines,

From high up on rugged hillsides,
Where jasmine perfumes the heights,
And in from those rocky reefs where
The Ligurian laps so light.

Here, overlooking the blue,
Verdant, vine-tangled terraces,
And clinging to steep slopes, pretty
Pastel-painted parishes.

Here the fishers and the shepherds
Sip on sweet Sciacchetrà,
These, now Dantes, now Petrarchs, and
Swallows whistle through the air.

And in sleepy Bonassola,
In that little rose chapel,
As in Byron's ghostly grotto,
Inspiration is ample.

Su Nuraxi

Millennia have passed by,
Long and tall grasses have grown,
And the world has forgotten,
Something that was once well known.

But the folk there never forgot,
What lay there beneath that hill,
They kept in their memory,
What was underneath it still.

Sifting through the sands of time,
The labour of giants appeared,
Boulders heaped up high by such
Men the world no longer rears.

Maecen … no, Herculean,
A wonder of yesteryear,
In Barumini's wastelands,
Oases of stone appeared.

Su Mannau

We wound our way 'long rivered routes, the
Sun beating down 'pon our backs,
To where that Avernian cave gapes
Wide, its yawning mouth so black.

Once inside, out of the blazing heat,
And far from the eyes of God,
We worked our way down winding routes where
Troglodyte and troll once trod.

Through galleries green and chambers tall,
With a cold draught on our backs,
We followed the trickling, gurgling sound,
Deeper down into the black.

And there we found some Stygian lake,
Its water crystal clear,
And we thought we'd find grim Charon's skiff
Lying moored upon that mere.

A vast cathedral then opened up,
Where the rock dripped down like wax,
A gothic grotto, glittering, and
Bats fluttering through the black.

A place being dug out by time, and God,
Moulded over and over again –
For ev'rything always changes, they say,
And naught ever stays the same –

But down there, even in those hellish haunts,
We saw that one thing does endure,
One thing that never, ever changes,
And that's God's sway over all.

Isola Rossa

Rocking about, to and fro,
I am bounced about the boat,
The sea's foaming up white and
Nausea foams up from my throat.

But the skipper has his sea legs,
And he's drawing in his nets,
A long and tiresome task, but
We wonder what's in there next.

Spiny *rascasse,* cuttlefish,
Careful fingers work them free,
Patiently he goes about
Gathering the sea's bounty.

O'er from Isola Rossa,
Where the water's clear and blue,
He hauls in his heavy traps
Where octopuses lie glued.

At the mercy of the sea,
He thus toils day after day,
But he never takes home much, and
Always less than yesterday.

Caprera

Down below those rocky crags,
Where the shepherds drive their flocks,
There're coves where the tide softly laps,
And the sailboats gently rock.

I plunge into the turquoise blue,
And the crystal waters part,
A whole new world comes into view,
And into this world I dart.

All slows right down and silence roars,
And I calmly make my way,
Ov'r shell-strewn stiles, through barnacled doors,
Where spiny urchins hold sway.

Warm and cool streams will carry me,
And along I gladly glide,
The little fishes deftly flee,
And beneath the rocks they hide.

But at length they return and greet
This outlandish visitor,
Who knew not what lay 'fore his feet,
But who now swims far from shore.

Camino de Santiago

From Burgos before first light,
With my staff and cockel hat,
Making for the Field o' Stars,
With ros'ry beads from my nan.

Following James' scallops,
Finding *albergues* and stamps,
The Milky Way high above,
And under its stars you'll camp.

Out into the Meseta,
Only kites for company,
Summer's heat upon your back,
Feeling nothing but lonely.

Out here the sound of silence,
Horizons stretch ever out,
You avoid the midday sun,
But you're still out when it goes down.

You had looked at everything,
Now you're counting ev'ry stone,
You had been thinking so deeply,
Now every thought is gone.

Tapas soon became *pintxos,*
And *pintxos, raciones.*
You find crayfish traps in streams,
And squid in *pulperías.*

And farms and monasteries,
In those sleepy villages,
And you sleep under haystacks,
And bathe in freezing rivers.

Legs ache and you feel dizzy,
But onwards you have to press,
You go past countless crosses,
But you're still making progress.

Green Galicia arrives,
That barren desert's behind,
Up misty hills you climb and
Eucalyptus woods you'll find.

The end of the 'Way' appears,
And like Charles, you are now there,
The Botafumeiro swings o'er,
And I leave my nan's beads here.

England, O England

The green, the green, a boundless scene,
Rises and falls o'er hills and denes.

And the white, the white, to left and to right,
Spring lambs next to their mothers' sides.

And the blue, the blue, a river snakes through,
Willows lined up in their weeping queues.

And the gold, the gold, a sight to behold
Those fragrant crops before farmers' homes.

~~~

And the hedgerow and the thicket,
The haystacks neatly packed,
Gentlemen playing cricket,
These things that my world lacks.
~~~

Everton

(In Scouse Dialect)

Off de footie today, our kid,
Goin' wid all me mates,
Catch de bus wid all de lads,
Singin' songs while we wait.

Singin' songs of our history,
De giants of our club,
Dixie Dean, de School o' Science,
Golden Vision and Big Dunc.

In de ale 'ouse for a bevvie,
Den chippie, bet, and go,
And thru de rusty turnstile,
Auld Lady's all in blue.

"And if u know your history,"
Gladys Street's in full song,
Den Z-Cars is a-ringing out,
De Blues are coming on.

All week we've been waiting for dis,
For three o'clock to come,
And now de whistle has been blown,
Dream till de game is done.

Bifter or loosie at halfies,
Spend me dosh on a jar,
A sarney, buttie, pie, or Scouse,
Know worra mean, la?

Watch dem knock about de casey,
Made up if we hammer dem,
I love a game of togger, me,
Dead good if we tonk dem.

Rambling

Over stiles, then mile after mile,
Towards the tavern we go,
Along the trail, along the dale,
Before the midwinter snows.

Past blackest hills, through bitter chill,
We're sloshing through swampy bogs,
Past felled trees, over rushing streams,
After our sheep-scaring dog.

Staff in hand churning up the land,
Putting filthy fields to plough,
Ewes take fright and hares take to flight,
As we head up to yonder brow.

Then heathered heights and soaring kites,
Over moors and fells we go,
Over windswept wastes we make haste,
Down into the wood below.

Take short strides over mountainsides,
Think of open fires and ale,
Forget fatigue and all those leagues,
That's how a mountain is scaled.

Storm Fear

(For Robert Frost)

Somewhere along the vale, a gusting gale
Whispers something soft but sure,
For soon swelling up, shattering teacups,
It comes roaring 'long the moors.

The timber shakes, the beams seem set to break,
As we lie helpless in bed,
The wraithlike wight comes in the dead of night,
To fill us with fear and dread.

Tightly we hold on, in each other's arms,
And listen, and hope, and pray,
In Nature's tight grip, fickle fates are fixed,
Lest God whisks this wind away.

Marrakesh

Up out from the desert,
Before those snow-capped peaks
A red city rises,
A genie wakes from sleep.

Passing through Bab Agnaou,
Inside the city walls,
Through the old medina,
Into Jemaa el-Fnaa.

Bustling with life, colour,
A maze of *souks* beyond,
You take a look around,
At just what this world spawns.

Mystics and magicians,
Snake charmers, acrobats,
Camels and monkeys, and
Tourists in panamas.

Tambourines and drums beat,
And pipes and *ouds* are played,
Here're lanterns, there're rugs, and
In tagines couscous's made.

Trays of lemons, chillies,
Capers, olives, pickles,
Mint, and dried fruit and nuts,
And ev'ry single smell.

Up out from the desert,
Before those snow-capped peaks
A red city rises,
A genie wakes from sleep.

The Amazon

A snaking river rushes by,
Its ripples glist'ning under the sky,
Verdant trees are either side,
As I sit looking on.

The clouds are passing overhead,
The blue is quickly turning deep red,
All the birds have by now fled,
And I sit looking on.

The night has fallen on this scene,
The insects buzz about in their teams,
Above, bats circling are seen,
While I am looking on.

The sounds of night from over there,
But the world keeps spinning, doesn't care,
This the life for those who dare,
But I'm still looking on …

About the Author

Dr. Paul T. M. Jackson is a graduate with bachelor's and master's degrees in classics, a master's degree in teaching and learning, and a PhD in ancient philosophy that he passed with no corrections under examination by A.G. Leventis Professor of Greek Culture at the University of Cambridge Tim Whitmarsh and the Open University's Dr. Carolyn Price.

He is a qualified teacher of religious education and has several years experience as a head of classics in the United Kingdom and as a teacher of literature in France. He also has several academic publications, including "The Gods of Philodemus" in the *Rosetta Journal* and "The Polytheism of the Epicureans" in *Walking the Worlds*, and has reviewed Marchand & Verde's *Épicurisme et Scepticisme* for Cambridge University Press and Ovid's *Heriodes* for OCR / Bloomsbury Academic UK. He is associated with numerous professional societies and institutions and has enjoyed research stays, such as at the Fondation Hardt in Geneva.

His travel diary, *A Greek Odyssey*, was published in 2018 through Wanderlust, and his translation of Alexandre Dumas' sprawling epic *Isaac Laquedem* will be later on in the year. His translations of French poetry have also recently appeared in *Better than Starbucks*.

About The Poetry Box®

The Poetry Box® was founded in 2011 by Shawn Aveningo & Robert R. Sanders, who wholeheartedly believe that every day spent with the people you love, doing what you love, is a moment in life worth cherishing. Their boutique press celebrates the talents of their fellow artisans and writers through professional book design and publishing of individual collections, as well as their flagship literary journal, *The Poeming Pigeon*.

Feel free to visit the online bookstore (thePoetryBox.com), where you'll find more titles including:

Verse on the Vine: A Celebration of Community, Art, Poetry & Wine

Keeping It Weird: Poems & Stories of Portland, Oregon

The Way a Woman Knows by Carolyn Martin

Of Course, I'm a Feminist! edited by Ellen Goldberg

Giving Ground by Lynn M. Knapp

Broadfork Farm by Tricia Knoll

The Poeming Pigeon: A Literary Journal of Poetry

Psyche's Scroll by Karla Linn Merrifield

and more . . .